COMPREHENSION SKILLS

CONCLUSION

LEVEL C

D1072903

Linda Ward Beech

Tara McCarthy

Donna Townsend

STECK-VAUGHN
ELEMENTARY · SECONDARY · ADULT · LIBRARY

A Harcourt Company

www.steck-vaughn.com

Editorial Director:	Diane Schnell
Project Editor:	Anne Souby
Associate Director of Design:	Cynthia Ellis
Design Manager:	Cynthia Hannon
Media Researcher:	Christina Berry
Production:	Rusty Kay
Cover Illustration:	Stephanie Carter
Cover Production:	Alan Klemp
Photograph:	Jack Demuth

ISBN 0-7398-2638-7

8 9 0 BNG 04

To draw a conclusion, you have to be a detective. You must put all the clues together in order to find the answer.

Look at the picture. The man is working. What is his job? Suppose you knew that people with his job work on engines. Would that be a clue about his job? Which parts of the picture give you clues about his job?

What Is a Conclusion?

A conclusion is a decision you make after thinking about what you have read. In a story the writer may not state all of his or her ideas. When you read, you often have to hunt for clues so that you can understand the whole story. By putting all of the writer's clues together, you can draw a conclusion about something that the writer has not stated.

There are many stories in this book. You will draw conclusions based on each story that you read.

Try It!

Read this story about a rain forest. Think about what it tells you.

> The climate around the equator is always warm. Much of the land is covered with rain forests. It rains in these areas every day. Some land gets more than five hundred inches a year. September and March are the wettest and warmest times of the year.

What conclusion can you draw? Write your conclusion on the lines.

_____

_____

You might have written something such as "It is warm and wet in the rain forests" or "It is never cold in the rain forests." You can draw these conclusions from the paragraph. The first sentence tells about the warm climate around the equator. The second sentence says that it rains every day. From those clues, you can draw these conclusions.

Using What You Know

Let's say that animals can talk. Several animals are describing themselves in the stories below. Hunt for clues that tell which animal is talking. Answer the questions by writing the name of each animal.

I have black and white stripes. The horse is my cousin. I live in a herd and like to graze on grass. I live on the huge plains of Africa. When I'm frightened, I run away as fast as I can. I can run forty miles per hour.

What am I? _____

I'm the largest animal on land. I weigh 250 pounds at birth. I'm gray and have large ears. I'm also one of the smartest animals. I live in a group. If a member of my group gets hurt, I try to help. I eat and drink with my long trunk.

What am I? _____

I'm the tallest animal in the world. I could easily look into your second-story window. My long neck lets me eat the fruit and leaves that no other animal can reach. Lions, cheetahs, and hyenas are my enemies.

What am I? _____

I live in the ocean. The whale is my cousin. I have a long, pointed nose. I'm very intelligent, and I'm friendly to people. In fact, sometimes I even let people ride on my back. I'm playful and like to learn tricks. I'm often trained to perform for crowds.

What am I? _____

To check your answers, turn to page 60.

Practice Drawing Conclusions

This book asks you to draw conclusions by using the clues in the stories. Look at the example below.

◆

In 1958 there was an earthquake in Springhill, Canada. There were 69 men trapped in the mine near town. The rescue workers dug fast and hard. But by the sixth day, few family members came to the mine. The sad rescue workers shook their heads but kept on digging. Then a voice was heard through an air pipe. "There are 12 of us in here. Please rescue us."

__*B*__ 1. From this story you can tell that
  A. Springhill was a big city
  B. the people thought the men were dead
  C. it was snowing during the earthquake
  D. no one cared about the miners

The correct answer is **B**. The story says, "But by the sixth day, few family members came to the mine. The sad rescue workers shook their heads but kept on digging." From these clues you can conclude that the men were not expected to be found alive.

Sometimes a question will ask about something that you *cannot* tell from a story. Read the example that follows.

◆

Llamas are members of the camel family. But they look more like sheep. They have long necks and big ears. They live in the Andes Mountains. The owners get wool, meat, and milk from the llamas.

_____ 2. From this story you <u>cannot</u> tell
  A. where llamas live
  B. what owners get from the llamas
  C. how many years llamas live
  D. what llamas look like

To check your answer, turn to page 60.

How to Use This Book

Read the stories in this book. Then answer the questions.

You can check your answers yourself. If you wish, tear out pages 61 and 62. Find the unit you want to check. Fold the answer page on the dotted line. It will show the correct unit. Line up the answer page with your answers. Write the number of correct answers in the score box at the top of the page.

Remember that each question has one correct answer. Sometimes you may think that two of the answers are correct. If that happens, read the story again. Then choose the better answer.

Hints for Better Reading

◆ Read all the clues in the story. Write the clues in your own words.

◆ Find a conclusion that fits all the clues. To make sure that you find the correct conclusion, ask yourself, "How do I know this?" You should know because of the clues in the story.

Challenge Yourself

Read each story. Then answer the questions. At least one of the answers is a conclusion that you can draw from the story. Write another conclusion that you can draw.

Writing

On pages 30–31 and 58–59, there are stories with questions. These do not have answers for you to choose. Think of an answer. Write it in your own words. You will find suggested answers on page 60. But your answers may be different.

1. Jay and Jean went to the store to buy toys for their baby. "Let's get a toy cat that has painted eyes," said Jay. "Button eyes can fall off, and the baby might eat them." They also wanted a wooden train set. Jean made sure that the train didn't have any sharp edges. They also bought a set of paints. The paints were marked *Safe for all ages.* Jay and Jean knew that their baby would like these toys.

2. People are always thinking of new things to sell in machines. Most machines sell snacks and drinks. But now machines even sell flowers. Machines are placed where many people will see them. For instance, lunchrooms are a good place to put snack machines. Baseball parks are a good place for drink machines.

3. Carla woke up when the rooster crowed. She lit a candle. Then she built a fire in the fireplace. The fire would help her make a good, warm breakfast. When Juan woke up, Carla sent him to gather more firewood. Juan also brought water from the well. After he ate, Juan walked the horses to the field to plow.

4. Purim is a Jewish holiday that honors Esther. Esther was a queen who lived hundreds of years ago. She saved the lives of her people. Today Purim is a time for eating and drinking. Children put on plays, and people read Esther's story.

5. Ella Fitzgerald was a great jazz singer. She began singing by accident, or so the story goes. When she was 15, she entered a contest. She planned to dance, but her knees shook too much. She decided to sing instead. A player in a famous band heard her. He brought her to sing with his band for one night. She sang with bands for the rest of her life!

_____ **1.** From this story you can tell that
    A. Jean was a painting teacher
    B. Jean liked the train set the best
    C. Jean and Jay bought only safe toys
    D. Jean wanted a train with sharp edges

_____ **2.** From this story you can tell that
    A. drinks from a machine taste best
    B. some machines sell things besides food
    C. all drink machines are found in baseball parks
    D. machines are placed where people won't
       see them

_____ **3.** From this story you can tell that
    A. Carla and Juan have many cows
    B. Carla and Juan have six children
    C. Carla and Juan probably live on a farm
    D. Carla and Juan plow the fields together

_____ **4.** From this story you can tell that
    A. Esther was probably very pretty
    B. Esther lived a hundred years ago
    C. there was no Purim before Esther lived
    D. Jewish people don't like Esther

_____ **5.** You can conclude that
    A. Fitzgerald should have been a dancer
    B. the player who heard her liked dancing
    C. Fitzgerald sang at churches
    D. Fitzgerald was a good singer

1. Baseball is a big sport in Japan. The rules are the same as those in America. But the customs are different. Players in Japan don't show their anger when they're *out*. They don't try to hurt the player from the other team as the player slides into second base. Also, when the fans clap, the players bow to them.

2. The knight in chess is different from the other pieces. The knight is the only piece that can jump over the other ones. This move comes from the days of the knights. Knights traveled far and wide in search of adventure. They traveled off the regular road. There they often met enemies. The knight in chess also does not have a regular move. The knight's move in chess is like the life of the knight of long ago.

3. Long ago, Spanish ships sailed to America. They landed in a warm part of the country. The sun shone brightly there. Flowers bloomed even in the winter. There wasn't any snow. The Spanish people called the land Florida. It is the Spanish word for "blooming." That's how the state got its name.

4. Years ago in England, many people became sick. Nobody knew why. Then a doctor found out that all the sick people lived near each other. He noticed that they all drank water from the same water well. The doctor took the handle off the well pump. People could no longer draw and drink the water. Suddenly they stopped getting sick.

5. How fast can you run? At top speed a human can run about 20 miles per hour. A snake can travel 2 miles per hour. The fastest mammal is the cheetah. It can run up to 70 miles per hour. But a golden eagle can fly 120 miles per hour. And a duck hawk can fly up to 180 miles per hour.

_____ **1.** From this story you can tell that
    A. Japanese players do not slide into second base
    B. American players show their anger
    C. Japanese players can play better
    D. Japanese players wave when the fans clap

_____ **2.** From this story you can tell that
    A. all chess pieces move in the same way
    B. the knight in chess has a regular move
    C. chess pieces move in different ways
    D. the knight in chess does not move

_____ **3.** From this story you can tell that
    A. American states can have Spanish names
    B. the Spanish people came in the spring
    C. *Florida* means "snow" in Spanish
    D. the Spanish ships landed in Texas

_____ **4.** From this story you can tell that
    A. everyone in England got sick
    B. the doctors at that time were not very smart
    C. the water was making the people sick
    D. there weren't enough doctors to help the sick

_____ **5.** From this story you can tell that
    A. eagles fly faster than duck hawks
    B. snakes move very fast
    C. cheetahs run faster than humans
    D. humans are the fastest mammals

1. The people in one town didn't like the nearby highway. Its turns were very sharp. Many people had been killed on that road. It began to be called Highway to Heaven. The people put some wrecked cars on top of poles near the road. They also lit up the cars at night. People still drive the Highway to Heaven. But now they are much more careful.

2. The warm sun shines on the sea. The sun's heat turns some of the sea water into a fine mist. The mist rises and forms clouds. Then the water falls back to Earth. The water fills rivers and lakes. In time the water runs back to the sea. The whole thing starts over again, just like a circle. There isn't any water added or lost.

3. Where is the safest place to be when lightning strikes? Lightning often strikes the tallest thing around. A tree is more likely to be hit than is the flat ground. So if it rains, don't stand under a tree. Don't stand in an open field either. Stay inside of a building or in your car during a storm. But don't touch any metal until after the storm.

4. One day John Penne drove by the hospital. He was surprised to see the number of people waiting by the street. Some were sick. Others were weak. All were waiting for a ride home. John wondered about these people. He decided to help them. Now he stops his car at the hospital and offers rides. He will give a free ride to anyone who needs one.

5. Many birds migrate. They fly south in the winter. In the summer they return to the north. The bird that makes the longest trip is the Arctic tern. The tern's summer breeding grounds are found in the Arctic. The bird flies south to spend the winter in Antarctica. The trip covers more than ten thousand miles each way.

_____ **1.** From this story you can tell that
    A. people always drove slowly on the highway
    B. the wrecked cars were a warning to drivers on the highway
    C. people always got robbed on the highway
    D. people stopped driving on that highway

_____ **2.** From this story you can tell that
    A. the amount of water on Earth stays the same
    B. the oceans will dry up some day
    C. the water in rivers runs away from the sea
    D. the mist causes lightning

_____ **3.** From this story you can tell that
    A. lightning never strikes the same place twice
    B. lightning hits cars first and buildings second
    C. some places are safer than others in a storm
    D. it's safe to fly a kite during a storm

_____ **4.** From this story you can tell that
    A. Penne drives many people home
    B. Penne charges $6 for a ride
    C. Penne takes people to the movies
    D. Penne does not care about helping others

_____ **5.** You can tell from the story that the Arctic tern
    A. does not migrate
    B. flies over twenty thousand miles each year
    C. breeds in Antarctica
    D. flies south to the Arctic each summer

1. At first it was difficult for Kent to ask for help. Later he looked forward to meeting with his teacher. Kent was happy to be learning what he needed to know. He was able to talk to his teacher as a friend.

2. Sid paid his fare and found a seat. He looked out the window as he passed street after street. When a woman with a baby got on, he got up and gave her his seat. He was glad that his ride was short.

3. Fran marked her place and then closed the book. She put it on the table next to her bed. Then she fluffed up the pillow and set the alarm clock. She checked the window to make sure it was open. Then she crawled under the covers and fell asleep.

4. Bonnie went to the post office to buy some stamps. But they didn't have the kind of stamps she wanted. So Bonnie bought another kind and mailed her letters. Then she went to the bank to get some wrappers for pennies. A worker told her that they were out of penny wrappers. So Bonnie decided to roll up her pennies on another day.

5. A fisherman brought a large fish to the king and was paid well for it. As the fisherman left, he picked up a valuable coin off the floor. The angry king called the man back. "That was not yours," he said. "I was afraid that someone would step on the king's face," the man said. The king liked the man's answer and let him keep the coin.

_____ **1.** In this story Kent has become
     A. sleepy
     B. trusting
     C. suspicious
     D. afraid

_____ **2.** You can tell that Sid is
     A. on a plane
     B. in a taxi
     C. on a bus
     D. on a boat

_____ **3.** You can conclude that Fran
     A. finished reading her book
     B. wanted some fresh air in the room
     C. works in an office
     D. leaves the porch light on at night

_____ **4.** Bonnie's two errands were alike because
     A. she walked to both places
     B. she bought something in both places
     C. she used pennies in both places
     D. neither place had what she wanted

_____ **5.** The fisherman's answer showed that
     A. someone was going to step on the king's face
     B. the king's picture was on the coin
     C. the fisherman was afraid of the king
     D. the king was afraid of the fisherman

1. About two hundred years ago, a doctor climbed a mountain in Europe. In those days people never climbed mountains. They did not know what the tops of mountains were like. In fact they thought the doctor would meet many terrible monsters along the way. He came back down, safe and sound. He hadn't seen a single monster. Today many people enjoy the sport of mountain climbing.

2. Ants help keep one tree in South America safe. This tree has thorns that are hollow. The ants live inside the thorns. When animals try to eat the tree's leaves, the ants rush out from the thorns. Hundreds of ants bite the animal. The thorns also stick the animal until it moves away.

3. Long ago in Europe, there were no police. Instead there were only town watchpersons. A watchperson walked the streets at night. Troublemakers stayed away. A watchperson walked for a length of time called a watch. Then someone else took over the next watch. How did a watchperson know when to stop walking? The watchperson carried a small clock. Today the name of the small clock reminds us of the watchpersons of Europe.

4. Baby Dee woke up and started crying loudly. Scott ran to her from the kitchen. He held Dee and talked to her. Scott didn't know why she was crying. He had fed Dee earlier. He checked to see if the baby's clothes were wet. But they were dry. Then Scott noticed an open safety pin lying in Dee's bed.

5. The largest fish on Earth is the whale shark. This giant shark can grow twice as large as an elephant. The whale shark can weigh up to 12 tons. But this shark is not harmful to people. It survives by eating only small water plants and animals.

_____ **1.** From this story you can tell that
    A. there are monsters living on mountains
    B. there were trees on top of the mountain
    C. others began climbing mountains after the doctor returned
    D. the doctor was hurt during his climb

_____ **2.** From this story you can tell that
    A. the tree and the ants need each other
    B. ants eat other animals for food
    C. the tree in this story is very tall
    D. the thorns don't hurt the animals

_____ **3.** From this story you can tell that
    A. a length of time was called a stretch
    B. the name of the clock is timer
    C. the name of the clock is watch
    D. the watchpersons ran races on the streets

_____ **4.** From this story you can tell that
    A. the baby was probably very hungry
    B. the safety pin probably hurt Dee
    C. Scott had to take care of only one child
    D. Scott was not a good father

_____ **5.** The story suggests that the whale shark
    A. is larger than an elephant
    B. attacks people
    C. is smaller than an elephant
    D. is not a fish

1. Most desert plants have sharp stickers. These spines help the desert plant drink water. Morning mist forms big drops on these stickers. When the drops fall, the plant drinks the water. The spines also make the hot desert winds circle around the plant. This keeps the wind from taking the plant's water.

2. The War of 1812 was a strange war. It started when British ships stopped some American ships. The angry Americans warned the British to be careful. The British agreed to stop making so much trouble. But there were no telephones at that time. So the news didn't get to America very quickly. Just two days after the British agreed to stop causing trouble, the Americans started the war.

3. The faces of rulers appear on English coins. But each new ruler faces in a different direction from the ruler before him or her. This practice began more than three hundred years ago. At that time Charles II was king. He did not like the ruler before him. So he ordered that his face point in the opposite direction on the coins. This practice has continued through the years.

4. "Don't jump!" the firefighters shouted. The woman stood at a window on the eleventh floor. The fire burned behind her. She was very scared. The firefighters climbed to the twelfth floor. One of them found an old hose in the hallway. "Tie this to me," he said. "I'll climb out the window. She'll see that we're near, and maybe she won't jump." Because of this the woman's life was saved.

5. The oldest trees on Earth are in the pine family. They are known as bristlecone pines. These pines can be found high in the White Mountains. These mountains are found in California. Some of these trees are more than four thousand years old.

_____ **1.** From this story you can tell that
   A. most desert plants need spines to live
   B. the spines on desert plants do not help them
   C. desert plants do not live very long
   D. the wind does not blow in the desert

_____ **2.** From this story you can tell that
   A. telephones might have kept the war from starting
   B. the Americans liked fighting wars back then
   C. the Americans did not have very many ships
   D. the Americans never warned the British

_____ **3.** From this story you can tell that
   A. Charles II began a new practice
   B. all English coins look alike
   C. Charles II liked the ruler before him
   D. English coins are made from old mirrors

_____ **4.** From this story you can tell that
   A. the fire was on the twelfth floor of the building
   B. the jump would have killed the woman
   C. the woman had to go to the hospital
   D. the woman wasn't scared at all

_____ **5.** The story tells that bristlecone pines
   A. do not live very long
   B. grow very tall
   C. are found at a high altitude
   D. grow in Canada

1. Dr. Camuti treated sick cats. He often went to their homes. One day a red-haired woman asked him to look at her big orange cat. The cat hid under the bed when it heard the doctor coming. Dr. Camuti and the woman crawled under the bed to catch the cat. He shouted, "I've got the cat!" But the woman yelled, "Ouch!"

2. Harold and June planted corn, beans, and carrots. June planted marigolds nearby. "I'm glad that marigold plants help keep the bugs away from the other plants," she said. "Just keep the vegetables away from the black walnut tree," Harold said. "Last year we planted seeds near it. Hardly anything came up there. But the rest of the garden did well."

3. The baby came home from the hospital. But Ken did not like his new baby brother. "Take it back! You got a new baby because I'm not good enough for you!" Ken yelled. Ken's parents talked with him for a long time. They told him that the baby would need special care at first. But that didn't mean they didn't love Ken anymore. This made him feel much better. He even held the baby in his arms.

4. Joey baked some cornbread. He mixed cornmeal, flour, eggs, milk, baking powder, and butter. Then he put the cornbread in the oven for thirty minutes. When it was done, it was two inches high. Joey liked it so much that he made some more cornbread. But this time he forgot to mix in the baking powder. The cornbread came out flat. It looked like a tortilla!

5. The largest hole ever dug is found in South Africa. It was dug as a diamond mine. The digging continued for 43 years. The miners removed 22 million tons of rock and clay. But they found almost a ton of diamonds! Today the mine is used as a museum.

_____ **1.** From this story you can tell that
    A. the orange cat hid under the bed often
    B. the doctor didn't like orange cats
    C. the doctor grabbed the woman's hair
    D. the orange cat was glad to see the doctor

_____ **2.** From this story you can tell that
    A. the bugs liked to eat the marigolds
    B. some plants can help or hurt other plants
    C. marigolds are red and orange bugs
    D. many vegetables grew near the walnut tree

_____ **3.** From this story you can tell that
    A. Ken didn't feel loved anymore
    B. the new baby was mad at Ken and his parents
    C. the new baby cried all the time
    D. Ken didn't like his new baby sister

_____ **4.** From this story you can tell that
    A. Joey had never baked cornbread before
    B. the baking powder made the cornbread rise
    C. cornbread was Joey's favorite thing to cook
    D. Joey made tortillas often

_____ **5.** You can tell from the story that
    A. the miners did not dig very long
    B. they dug a hole only three feet deep
    C. the miners found just a few diamonds
    D. they found more rock and clay than diamonds

1. Many people don't like bugs. Some bugs bite or sting people. Other bugs eat people's plants and fruits. People poison bugs to get rid of them. Now scientists are finding new ways to kill bugs with germs. The germs make the bugs sick, and then they die. Scientists also use some bugs to fight the other bugs. The ladybug is an example. It eats bugs that hurt fruit.

2. Laughing makes people feel great. Some people think that laughing is the best thing in life. Now scientists have shown that laughing is good for the body, too. Laughing makes the heart beat faster. It brings more air into the body. Many people keep fit by running. But laughing is easier on the feet!

3. How do people put out forest fires? Machines are used to knock down trees that aren't burning. Other machines remove the fallen trees. This clears some of the land. The fire can't cross this land because there is nothing to burn. The firefighters also start small fires nearby to clear more land. Airplanes help put out the bigger fires by pouring clay on them.

4. Mark Twain was a famous writer. One night he was going to give a talk in a small town. He went to the barbershop to get a shave. The barber asked, "Are you going to hear that famous writer tonight? It's sold out, you know. If you go, you'll have to stand." "Just my luck," said Twain. "I always have to stand when that man gives a talk!"

5. Have you ever heard people call money by the name of bits? There was once a Mexican coin called a bit. It was worth 12 1/2 cents. This coin was also used in parts of the United States. So the people began calling American coins by the name of bits, too. Today a quarter is sometimes known as two bits. A half-dollar is called four bits.

_____ **1.** From this story you can tell that

    A. poison is not the only way to get rid of bugs

    B. people need to stay away from ladybugs

    C. most bugs like to eat fruit trees

    D. the germs make the bugs stronger

_____ **2.** From this story you can tell that

    A. laughing is good for your health

    B. swimming is very good for your body

    C. crying is like laughing

    D. laughing makes the heart beat slower

_____ **3.** From this story you can tell that

    A. it is easy to stop a big fire

    B. clay burns very easily when it gets hot

    C. there are many ways to fight forest fires

    D. firefighters make big fires to clear more land

_____ **4.** From this story you can tell that

    A. the barber did not like to hear writers talk

    B. the barber wasn't going to the talk

    C. the barber didn't know he was shaving Twain

    D. the barber only cut hair

_____ **5.** From this story you can conclude that

    A. Mexican coins are used in the United States

    B. today a bit is worth less than a nickel

    C. the name of the Mexican coin is still used
       for money

    D. Mexican coins are now used for horse bridles

1. Wilbur Voliva believed that Earth was flat. He said that the sun was only three thousand miles away. He didn't believe that the sun was millions of miles away. In fact, Voliva didn't believe anything that scientists said. He also wanted to prove them wrong. So each year Voliva offered a big money prize. It was for anyone who could prove him wrong and show that the world was round.

2. Doctors noticed that some sick people had had changes in their lives. Something new had happened to them. A few had new homes or jobs. Others had just married. Changes of any kind seemed to make these people weaker. And it was easy for germs to make them sick.

3. Dan and Lola are married to each other. Both of them are truck drivers. They like driving trucks. They think that most truck drivers are fine people. But they also think that truck drivers have a bad name. So Dan and Lola are working to get some laws passed. These laws would make truck drivers who drive too fast stay off the road.

4. The town was on fire. Jim Root was the train engineer. He knew that the fire would burn the station and all the people on the train! So he started the train to get it out of town. But the worst part of the fire lay in front of him. So he drove the train backwards the whole way. Finally the train reached a lake outside of town. Root had saved everybody's life!

5. People say that they see a person's face when they look up at the moon. But in China the people say that they see something different. They see a toad or a rabbit. The Chinese celebrate the moon's birthday. This event takes place on September 15. Cakes are baked and covered with candy toads and rabbits. The moon's birthday marks the end of the harvest.

_____ **1.** From this story you can tell that
    A. Voliva thought that Earth was round
    B. scientists thought that the sun was millions of miles away
    C. Voliva believed everything that scientists said
    D. Voliva knew much about the sun

_____ **2.** From this story you can tell that
    A. people who live in old houses stay healthy
    B. changes can make some people sick
    C. newly married people never get sick
    D. people get well with germs

_____ **3.** From this story you can tell that
    A. many truck drivers are married to each other
    B. some truck drivers drive too fast
    C. most truck drivers carry food to other places
    D. most truck drivers are bad people

_____ **4.** From this story you can tell that
    A. the last car on the train burned up
    B. Jim had never driven a train before
    C. the train could not be turned around
    D. the lake was near the train station

_____ **5.** You can tell that the Chinese
    A. have different customs about the moon
    B. think that the moon is 15 years old
    C. like to ruin good cakes
    D. don't know much about the moon

1. Mrs. King wanted to have a party. Her son also wanted to invite all of his friends. "But the living room is too small," said Mrs. King. "Not everyone will fit." Her son had an idea. First they painted the walls white. Then they covered one wall with mirrors. Finally they put big red pillows on the floor. The first friend who arrived said, "This room looks huge!"

2. The plant with the biggest seed in the world is called the coconut of the sea. Its huge seed can grow to be as big as a beach ball. It can weigh as much as fifty pounds.

3. Let's say that you wanted to write down all the words while someone was talking. It would be very hard. People talk much faster than they write. But you could learn a special kind of writing. It's called shorthand. Shorthand doesn't look at all like the writing in this book. For instance, a straight line stands for *am*. So you'd have to learn to read shorthand, too.

4. Nellie Bly worked for a newspaper. She managed to report stories that nobody else could. Once she wanted to know how doctors treated people who were poor. So she dressed in rags and pretended to be sick. She told them that she didn't have any money. She was taken to a hospital for the poor. There she had to sleep on the floor and eat terrible food. Later Nellie Bly wrote a story about her stay at this hospital. Her story surprised many people.

5. Grace could hardly wait until the fall. In fact, she was packed and ready to go. When the school year began, she would be in America. She would stay there for the full year. She felt lucky that she had been picked to study away from home. She would live with a family in Maine. Grace just knew she would like Maine.

_____ **1.** From this story you can tell that
    A. white walls can make rooms look bigger
    B. the Kings liked dark colors best
    C. the Kings were always having parties
    D. all their friends slept on the red pillows

_____ **2.** From this story you can tell that
    A. this plant probably grows in the United States
    B. this seed wouldn't make a good beach ball
    C. the seed is the size of a big orange
    D. the seed tastes like coconut

_____ **3.** From this story you can tell that
    A. today many people are learning shorthand
    B. shorthand is very easy to learn
    C. the word _the_ looks different in shorthand
    D. people talk more slowly than they write

_____ **4.** From this story you can tell that
    A. some hospitals were not kind to people who were poor
    B. Bly got sick when she was in the hospital
    C. Bly won a prize for writing the story
    D. the food at the hospital for the poor was good

_____ **5.** You can tell from the story that
    A. Grace is a good student
    B. Grace does not live in America
    C. Maine has many good schools
    D. Grace will not miss her family

1. In the early days, ranchers drove their cattle north to the train yards. The cattle drives covered many long, hot miles. One steer led some of these drives for eight years. His name was Old Blue. When the cowboys whistled, Old Blue started walking. When they pointed, Old Blue knew in which direction to walk. Old Blue wore a bell around his neck. The cows followed the sound of his bell.

2. During a war, finding workers can be hard. But one company didn't have any trouble. The owners asked their workers to work 12 hours each day. The owners paid them well. They also paid for the workers' meals. They offered free trips to the people who worked very hard. The workers worked well because they liked the company. The company also liked its workers.

3. Have you ever watched a pond freeze in winter? The water freezes first on the top. The ice forms a very thin sheet across the water. It takes only about twenty minutes for this sheet to form. Then slowly the ice begins to grow down toward the bottom. It takes an hour for the first sheet to become two times as thick.

4. Alexander Graham Bell spent much of his time helping people who could not hear. Both his mother and wife were deaf. The first telephone Bell made was to help people who were deaf. But it never did anything for the people that Bell wanted to help.

5. Toni Cade Bambara wrote books about African American life. *Gorilla, My Love* is a group of short stories. These stories are set in Harlem. Harlem is in New York City. The speakers in the book are all women. They are funny, strong, and truthful. All the stories show how important family is.

_____ **1.** From this story you can tell that
  A. ranchers didn't like to drive their cattle north
  B. Old Blue was so tame you could ride him
  C. Old Blue knew what the cowboys wanted
  D. Old Blue did a bad job

_____ **2.** From this story you can tell that
  A. people can't work more than eight hours a day
  B. people will work hard for high pay
  C. people do not like to take free trips
  D. people will not work hard during a war

_____ **3.** From this story you can tell that
  A. the bottom of the pond freezes first
  B. the fish in a cold pond all die after one hour
  C. the ice forms more slowly as it gets thicker
  D. the ice grows up toward the top

_____ **4.** From this story you can tell that
  A. Bell made the telephone to help his mother and wife
  B. the first telephone was made many years ago
  C. Bell could not hear very well either
  D. Bell spent much time helping people who were blind

_____ **5.** This story does <u>not</u> tell
  A. what Toni Cade Bambara wrote about
  B. where the characters in *Gorilla, My Love* live
  C. about Bambara's personal life
  D. about the speakers in *Gorilla, My Love*

1. Did you know you can start a campfire with ice? First find a large piece of very clear ice. Then melt it down in the palms of your hands. When it is ready, the ice should look like a lens. It should have smooth curves on both sides. Finally use the ice to direct the sun's rays onto paper or wood shavings. This will start the fire.

2. Nat Love was a special breed of man. He was a restless cowboy who helped settle the Wild West. As a young man, Love was a slave in Tennessee. Set free by the Civil War, Love learned to herd cattle. In Deadwood, South Dakota, Love won a big cowboy contest. There he gained his nickname, Deadwood Dick.

3. For years people longed to fly in space. They wanted to visit the moon. In 1957 the Soviet Union launched a satellite. Its name was *Sputnik*. The name means "fellow wayfarer." *Sputnik* was the first spacecraft to orbit Earth. *Sputnik* had no crew. But it paved the way for later space flights.

4. Most whales survive by eating small sea creatures known as krill. Some companies were planning to harvest krill. Mary Cahoon and Mary McWhinnie were afraid that this harvest would cause whales to starve. They went to the South Pole to study the problem. They were the first women to spend a whole winter at the cold South Pole.

5. Some early Native American tribes used adobe to build homes. Adobe is a sun-dried brick made of soil and straw. First they mixed soil and water to make mud. Next they added straw for strength. Then they put the mixture into a brick-shaped mold. Finally the brick was placed in the sun to dry. The dried bricks were used to build the walls of houses.

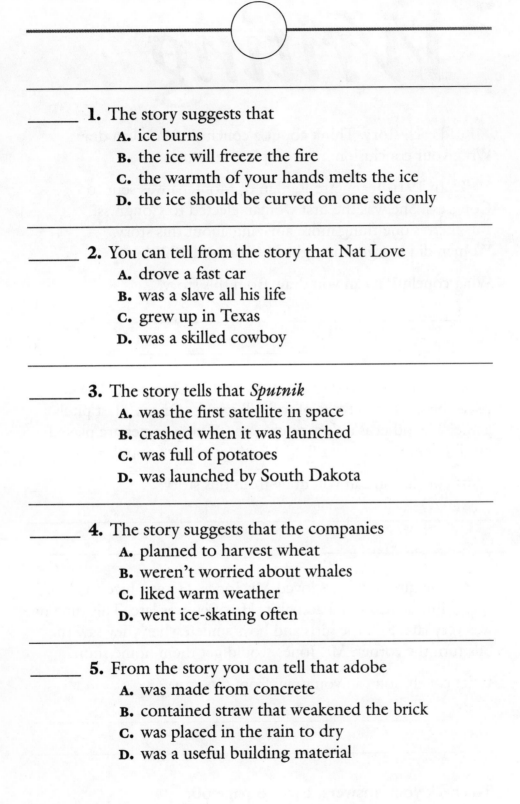

_____ **1.** The story suggests that
  A. ice burns
  B. the ice will freeze the fire
  C. the warmth of your hands melts the ice
  D. the ice should be curved on one side only

_____ **2.** You can tell from the story that Nat Love
  A. drove a fast car
  B. was a slave all his life
  C. grew up in Texas
  D. was a skilled cowboy

_____ **3.** The story tells that _Sputnik_
  A. was the first satellite in space
  B. crashed when it was launched
  C. was full of potatoes
  D. was launched by South Dakota

_____ **4.** The story suggests that the companies
  A. planned to harvest wheat
  B. weren't worried about whales
  C. liked warm weather
  D. went ice-skating often

_____ **5.** From the story you can tell that adobe
  A. was made from concrete
  B. contained straw that weakened the brick
  C. was placed in the rain to dry
  D. was a useful building material

Writing

Read each story. Think about a conclusion you can draw. Write your conclusion in a complete sentence.

1. In 1916 Jeannette Rankin of Montana was sent to Congress. She was the first woman elected to Congress. But there's one thing more amazing about this story. Women did not get the right to vote until 1920!

What conclusion can you draw from this story?

_____

_____

2. Softball is an old game. It started in Chicago in 1887. Now there are two types of softball games. One is a fast pitch game. The other is a slow pitch game. These games are played on different size playing fields. Both games are popular.

What conclusion can you draw from this story?

_____

_____

3. The girls and boys loved Mr. Jones. He was nice to all of them. But he had one bad habit. He often was late. This time he was very late. Still the girls and boys smiled when they saw the bus turn the corner. Mr. Jones would get them home soon.

What conclusion can you draw from this story?

_____

_____

To check your answers, turn to page 60.

Read the story below. What conclusions can you draw? Use the clues in the story to answer the questions in complete sentences.

The airplane ride took four hours. Laree's grandmother was waiting for her at the gate. Laree was glad to see her grandmother, but Midway Park was the real reason for the visit. She wanted to ride the Tytanic. It was supposed to be the biggest ride of its kind in the world. Laree knew she would get wet. She might even get soaked. Still she could not wait. Her school friends wanted to hear about the ride, and Laree planned to call them.

1. Was Laree's grandmother visiting her? How do you know?

_____

_____

2. Is Laree a student? How do you know?

_____

_____

3. Is the Tytanic a water ride? How do you know?

_____

_____

4. Do Laree's friends live near Laree's grandmother? How do you know?

_____

_____

To check your answers, turn to page 60.

1. Even though she had read the signs, Sally reached out her hand. She stretched forward with the popcorn at her finger tips. The soft mouth of the striped animal just fit through the bars and reached the popcorn. It nibbled greedily.

2. The shaggy, little animal went up to the back door. It rattled the screen door with its front paw and then sat down. It was quiet for a while. But soon a face appeared at the door, and then there was a scream of joy. "It's Goldie!" a girl's voice said. "She's come back."

3. In the morning Becky came downstairs. "I don't like this house at all," the girl told her parents. "It smells funny." Her mother asked if she had seen the wild strawberries that were growing in the front yard. Her father mentioned the pony he had seen at the neighboring house. The girl's eyes lit up.

4. The man tried to balance himself, but he wobbled. The wheels seemed to go in every direction at once. When he hit a bump, his foot lost its grip on the pedal. He put his feet on the ground. Then he let go of the handlebars and sat straight up on the narrow seat with his arms forward. "I haven't done this in a long time," he said with a laugh.

5. With short little strokes, Bernice first dabbed at the nose. Then she brushed near the ears. She wanted to finish the face before the sun set. She realized that she needed a deeper shadow under the man's eyes, so she dipped her brush again. She touched the canvas with the brush.

_____ **1.** You can tell that Sally
  A. is buying popcorn at the movies
  B. can't read the signs she has seen
  C. is feeding an animal at the zoo
  D. once owned the striped animal

_____ **2.** From this story you can tell that
  A. Goldie had lived at this house at one time
  B. the animal had never seen this house before
  C. the girl didn't know why the animal was there
  D. Goldie must be a dog

_____ **3.** You can conclude that this family
  A. is about to move to a new house
  B. has just moved into this house
  C. will leave the house because of Becky's feelings
  D. will punish Becky for being rude

_____ **4.** You can tell that the man is
  A. driving a car for the first time in a long time
  B. trying to use a mixer in the kitchen
  C. trying to ride a tricycle
  D. trying to ride a bicycle

_____ **5.** You can tell that Bernice
  A. works as a makeup artist
  B. works at a hospital
  C. is painting a picture of a man
  D. is cleaning an ancient mask

1. The water made a splashing sound as it ran past the big gray rocks. In some places it formed little pools. A small branch bobbed by as the water hurried down the hill. A skunk sat on the mossy bank and watched.

2. Flo and Mike were at the animal shelter. Flo wanted a kitten. Mike wanted a puppy. "Cats are cleaner," said Flo. "You don't have to give them baths or take them for walks." Mike didn't care about that. He thought that cats sleep too much to be good playmates.

3. When Tony woke up, he looked out the window. What luck! The mountain was covered with snow. Quickly he pulled on his long underwear and other warm clothes. He ate a good, hot breakfast so that he'd have plenty of energy. Then he checked his equipment. He clomped in his heavy boots toward the door and looked at the slopes.

4. Nina was walking down a long hall. She kept turning corners and looking for a certain door. But all the doors she found were the wrong ones. Suddenly a bell rang, and Nina thought, "Oh, I must run or I'll be late." But the bell kept ringing, and Nina couldn't run. Instead, she opened her eyes. The telephone beside her bed was ringing loudly.

5. A dog was carrying a bone in his mouth. As he walked over a bridge, he saw his reflection in the water. He thought it was another dog with another bone. "I'll bark and scare that dog away," he thought. "Then I'll have two bones!" After the dog barked, he found out that it doesn't pay to be greedy.

_____ **1.** You can tell that the skunk is sitting near
   A. a bathtub
   B. a fountain
   C. a stream
   D. a lake

_____ **2.** This story does <u>not</u> tell
   A. what Flo wanted
   B. what Mike wanted
   C. why Flo likes cats better than dogs
   D. what Flo and Mike decided to get

_____ **3.** In this story the mood is
   A. angry
   B. dangerous
   C. happy
   D. silly

_____ **4.** From this story you can tell that
   A. the telephone woke Nina from her dream
   B. Nina was in school
   C. Nina didn't want to answer the telephone
   D. Nina was glad the telephone rang

_____ **5.** The dog learned his lesson when
   A. the other dog ran away
   B. he had no bone at all
   C. he went home with a bone
   D. he jumped off the bridge

1. Ben stood in line at the counter waiting to pay for the things he had chosen. The air conditioning didn't work, and the store was hot. Ben was holding some heavy objects, and he wished the line would move faster. A woman went to the front of the line. People protested, but the woman didn't budge. Suddenly Ben put his things down and walked out of the store.

2. Kate took Celeste for a ride in her wagon. Kate pulled the wagon around the house, across the driveway, and over the lawn. As the wagon bumped along, Celeste fell out. At first Kate didn't notice, but then she looked back and saw Celeste lying on the grass. "Oh dear," Kate sighed as she walked over to pick up the smiling Celeste. "This always happens."

3. To test the temperature, Diana put her toe in the water. "Maybe I'll wait a while before going in," she thought. So she sat down and watched the sailboats near the opposite shore.

4. Something came at Simon in the dark. He slapped at it but missed. Again and again he was attacked. Although he tried, Simon was no match for his enemy. Sure enough, the next morning he had a red bump on his arm that itched.

5. A lion caught a mouse. "Please don't eat me!" begged the mouse. "Let me go, and I will do you a favor some day." The lion laughed, but he let the mouse go. Many days later some hunters caught the lion. They tied him up with ropes. After the hunters left, the mouse chewed the ropes and set the lion free.

_____ **1.** Ben walked out because
    A. he was tired of waiting
    B. the store was closing
    C. he was patient
    D. he was worried

_____ **2.** Celeste is probably Kate's
    A. sister
    B. cat
    C. doll
    D. cousin

_____ **3.** Diana is probably sitting on the shore of
    A. an ocean
    B. a bathtub
    C. a pool
    D. a lake

_____ **4.** You can conclude that Simon
    A. ran into poison ivy
    B. was attacked by a bear
    C. was chased by a dog
    D. was bitten by a bug

_____ **5.** The lion found out that
    A. mice are not good to eat
    B. hunters are harmless
    C. a little mouse is hard to catch
    D. little friends can do great deeds

1. Zora Neale Hurston wrote the story of her own life. It is called *Dust Tracks on the Road*. In it, she recorded speech very well. She wrote it as it was spoken. Her work helped people learn about African Americans in the past.

2. Valentina Tereshkova was nervous. She knew she'd soon make history. It was a still morning in 1963. She sat strapped in her seat. At last the Soviet spaceship began to shake. Its great engines roared. The ship climbed from the launch pad. It built up speed. Soon it was racing through the sky. Within minutes Valentina had become the first woman in space.

3. Stephen Hawking is a famous scientist. He has written books about physics and our universe. But Hawking must do all his work in a wheelchair. In his twenties he found out he had Lou Gehrig's disease. Later he lost his power to speak and write. Now he does his work on a special computer. The computer allows him to speak and type.

4. An apprentice is someone who works to learn a trade. The apprentice helps a skilled worker do a job. The helper learns the skill by doing it. Being a helper is a good way to learn a trade well. Many young people used to serve as apprentices. Some labor groups still use the apprentice plan.

5. Pompeii was a town near the volcano Mount Vesuvius. In A.D. 79 the volcano began to rumble. Then it erupted. A black cloud of smoke and ash rose from its cone. The strong blast caused buildings to sway and fall. Ash filled the sky, blotting out the sun. Thousands of people died from the blast. Then tons of ash settled on Pompeii. People could no longer live there. Pompeii became a ghost town.

◯

_____ **1.** This story does <u>not</u> tell
    A. where Zora Neale Hurston grew up
    B. what *Dust Tracks on the Road* is about
    C. that Hurston recorded speech well
    D. that Hurston wrote about her own life

_____ **2.** The story does <u>not</u> tell
    A. when Tereshkova made her flight
    B. how Tereshkova gained fame
    C. how long it took Tereshkova to become famous
    D. how many people went with Tereshkova

_____ **3.** The story suggests that Stephen Hawking
    A. is a baseball player
    B. uses a computer to walk
    C. can't use a regular typewriter
    D. likes to play video games

_____ **4.** You <u>cannot</u> tell from the story
    A. who an apprentice helps
    B. how long someone must be an apprentice
    C. if labor groups still use apprentices
    D. how an apprentice learns a skill

_____ **5.** The story tells that
    A. Vesuvius was a city
    B. the volcano's blast caused no damage
    C. Pompeii was located in Ireland
    D. the volcano caused people to leave Pompeii

1. A popular part of Yellowstone Park is Old Faithful. This geyser shoots out thousands of gallons of steam and water every hour. The water is heated deep in the ground. It works its way up through cracks in the ground. Then it bursts high into the air. Yellowstone Park has more geysers than anyplace else on Earth.

2. Evelyn Cheesman loved to study bugs. She worked as a helper in the Insect House at the London Zoo. In the 1920s she began to go on field trips. Most of her trips were to Asia. During her life she was able to collect forty thousand insects.

3. A great white building stands in Agra, India. It is called the Taj Mahal. It was built by a ruler named Shah Jahan. He wanted a special place to bury his dead wife. So twenty thousand men worked for twenty years to build the Taj Mahal.

4. Lewis Latimer was an African American man. When he was young, he learned the skill of drafting. Then he met Alexander Bell. Bell invented the telephone. He used a design drawn by Latimer. Not long after that, Latimer invented a special lamp. It was called the Latimer Lamp. Later he worked with the great inventor Thomas Edison.

5. Rosita put the flag up in front of her home. She had read about the correct way to do this. She knew that the flag can be flown from the top of a flag pole. She didn't have a flag pole, though. She also knew that the flag can be hung on a staff. That was how Rosita flew the flag.

_____ **1.** You <u>cannot</u> tell from the story
    A. how often Old Faithful erupts
    B. where Old Faithful can be found
    C. how the water is heated
    D. where Yellowstone Park is located

_____ **2.** The story suggests that Evelyn Cheesman
    A. was afraid of insects
    B. made most of her field trips to Africa
    C. worked with insects all her life
    D. did not collect insects

_____ **3.** You can tell that the Taj Mahal
    A. was built to be a grave
    B. is found in Indiana
    C. was built of granite
    D. took thirty years to build

_____ **4.** The story does <u>not</u> tell if Lewis Latimer
    A. learned drafting
    B. invented more than one thing
    C. worked with Thomas Edison
    D. invented a special lamp

_____ **5.** From this story you can tell that
    A. Rosita's flag is new
    B. Rosita lives in an apartment
    C. there is more than one right way to fly a flag
    D. Rosita lives in a house

1. Karen could not walk or dance. But she loved to move in her wheelchair while she listened to music. Her favorite singer was Elvis Presley. One day she decided she would become his pen pal. She wrote a letter to Elvis and mailed it. Days went by, and no reply came. At first Karen feared that Elvis might not write. But she kept hoping. At last the special letter came. It was the first of many.

2. Don't you wish you could break free of Earth's gravity? Then you could float in space. Spaceships have to break free of Earth's gravity to reach space. They must go very fast. In fact, they must travel at seven miles per second to break Earth's pull. That is about twenty-five thousand miles per hour.

3. As a lawyer Thurgood Marshall worked in many civil rights trials. He believed in "equal justice under the law." Marshall tried hard to gain that goal. He won many cases. He helped win equal rights for all Americans. Marshall's hard work paid off. First he was made a judge. Then he was picked to serve on the highest court in the land. He was made a Supreme Court justice. He became the first African American to hold that post.

4. In 1666 a great fire swept through London. At the time London was a crowded place. Many of its buildings were made of wood. The fire destroyed nearly the whole city. Thousands of homes were burned. Almost ninety churches were ruined. When London was rebuilt, stone was used instead of wood.

5. Salt is now a common spice. But long ago, salt was quite special. It was prized as a spice and as a medicine. Roman soldiers were given amounts of salt as extra pay. This pay was called salt money. From this term we got the word *salary*.

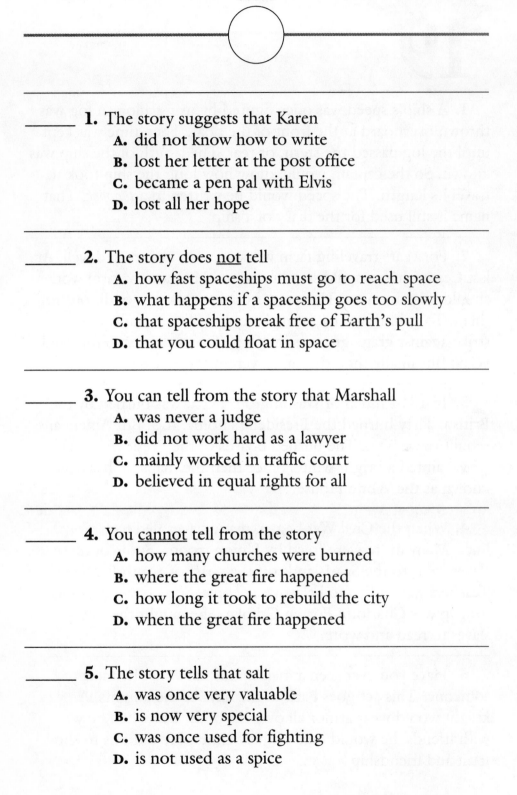

_____ **1.** The story suggests that Karen
    A. did not know how to write
    B. lost her letter at the post office
    C. became a pen pal with Elvis
    D. lost all her hope

_____ **2.** The story does <u>not</u> tell
    A. how fast spaceships must go to reach space
    B. what happens if a spaceship goes too slowly
    C. that spaceships break free of Earth's pull
    D. that you could float in space

_____ **3.** You can tell from the story that Marshall
    A. was never a judge
    B. did not work hard as a lawyer
    C. mainly worked in traffic court
    D. believed in equal rights for all

_____ **4.** You <u>cannot</u> tell from the story
    A. how many churches were burned
    B. where the great fire happened
    C. how long it took to rebuild the city
    D. when the great fire happened

_____ **5.** The story tells that salt
    A. was once very valuable
    B. is now very special
    C. was once used for fighting
    D. is not used as a spice

1. A ship's speed was once figured by using a log. A log was thrown overboard at the front of the boat. Then time was kept until the log passed the stern, or rear. The length of the ship was known. So the captain would know how long the ship took to travel its length. The speed would be written in a *logbook*. That name is still used for the diary of a ship.

2. For years traveling farm workers were not treated well. At last César Chávez could stand no more. He thought farm workers should be paid more. He wanted better working conditions for them. To gain these, he formed a union. The group went on strike against grape growers in 1965. The strike lasted for five years. But finally their demands were met.

3. In 1814 much of Washington, D.C., was burned by the British. They burned the President's home, too. But Americans rebuilt the capital. The burned boards of the President's home were painted a bright white. Since then the mansion has been known as the White House.

4. When the Civil War began, many slaves fled to Union lines. Many more were freed by Union troops. Some of these slaves went to the Sea Islands off the coast of South Carolina. Teachers were asked to help these people. Someone who went to help was Charlotte Forten Grimke. She taught the freed slaves to read and write.

5. Have you ever seen a man tip his hat when he meets someone? This act goes back to the days of the knights. A knight would wear armor all over his body. But when he was with friends, he would take off his helmet. He did this to show trust and friendship.

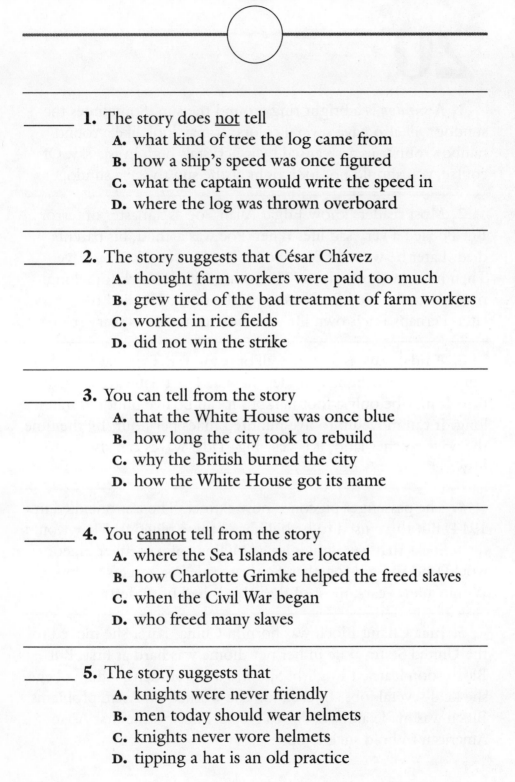

_____ **1.** The story does not tell
  A. what kind of tree the log came from
  B. how a ship's speed was once figured
  C. what the captain would write the speed in
  D. where the log was thrown overboard

_____ **2.** The story suggests that César Chávez
  A. thought farm workers were paid too much
  B. grew tired of the bad treatment of farm workers
  C. worked in rice fields
  D. did not win the strike

_____ **3.** You can tell from the story
  A. that the White House was once blue
  B. how long the city took to rebuild
  C. why the British burned the city
  D. how the White House got its name

_____ **4.** You cannot tell from the story
  A. where the Sea Islands are located
  B. how Charlotte Grimke helped the freed slaves
  C. when the Civil War began
  D. who freed many slaves

_____ **5.** The story suggests that
  A. knights were never friendly
  B. men today should wear helmets
  C. knights never wore helmets
  D. tipping a hat is an old practice

1. A *sundog* is a bright ring around the sun. Sometimes the sundog will also have several colors. It may look like a round rainbow. Sundogs are caused by ice crystals high in the sky. Of course, you should not look right at the sun to see a sundog.

2. Most readers know Edgar Allan Poe as a master of terror. But Poe led a very sad life. When Poe was a child, his parents died. Later he went to West Point, but he was asked to leave. Then he turned to writing. His young wife was sick for a long time. After she died Poe was never the same. He died two years later. Perhaps Poe's own life gave him ideas for his scary stories.

3. A tidal wave is a huge wall of sea water. This wave is often caused by an earthquake under the sea. The tidal wave is small at first. It may be only a foot tall, but it can be five hundred miles long. It can move up to five hundred miles per hour. By the time the wave reaches land, it is very big. Tidal waves can rise up to fifty feet.

4. The passenger pigeon is now extinct. The last one died in 1914. But there used to be billions of these pigeons. They would fly in flocks that were miles long. Millions of passenger pigeons would land and rest together. So they made easy targets for hunters. Within a few years, most of these birds had been destroyed.

5. Julia Chang Bloch was born in China. Later she moved to the United States. Life in her new home was hard at first. But Bloch soon learned English. She was a top student. After college she held several jobs. In each job she worked on Asian problems. Bloch was made ambassador to Nepal. She was the first Asian American to hold such a job.

_____ **1.** The story suggests that
   A. a sundog is an animal
   B. looking right at the sun can be harmful
   C. a sundog is caused by moonlight
   D. sundogs only occur in summer

_____ **2.** You <u>cannot</u> tell from the story if Poe
   A. went to West Point
   B. had an unhappy life
   C. wrote scary stories
   D. wrote any funny stories

_____ **3.** You can tell that tidal waves
   A. grow larger as they move toward shore
   B. move very slowly
   C. are only ten feet tall
   D. are caused by shipwrecks

_____ **4.** From this story you can tell that
   A. passenger pigeons rode on trains
   B. hunters killed most passenger pigeons
   C. passenger pigeons were hard to hunt
   D. only a few passenger pigeons remain

_____ **5.** The story does <u>not</u> tell
   A. where Bloch was born
   B. that Bloch held a job after college
   C. when Bloch moved to the United States
   D. to what country Bloch was ambassador

1. Francis Marion was a small, thin man. But he became a hero of the American Revolution. He set up his base in a South Carolina swamp. From there his soldiers launched raids on British camps. They caused the British troops all sorts of trouble. Marion's plans were always sly. Because of this he became known as the Swamp Fox.

2. Tooth care has always been important. The oldest known tooth care product was a "chew stick." It was used in Egypt five thousand years ago. This stick was rubbed on the teeth to clean them. Today's toothbrush has bristles. This type of brush was first used in China around A.D. 1500. Hog bristles were used at first. Now nylon bristles are used.

3. Franklin Roosevelt was President of the United States longer than anyone else. He was elected to the post four times. He helped pull the nation out of the Great Depression. He led the country through most of World War II. Franklin struggled with polio. At one point he lost the use of his legs. But with great effort, he gained back some use of his legs. His great courage made him one of the greatest Presidents.

4. Cora and her brother Floyd liked living in the city. They thought that city life was much more fun than country life. There were movies to see. There were parks to visit. There were museums and stores. The only thing they missed was having a horse.

5. When S.E. Hinton was 16, she wrote her first book, *The Outsiders*. It has since been made into a movie. Hinton says she started writing to fill a need. She wanted to write books that she herself would enjoy reading.

_____ **1.** From this story you can tell
        A. when the American Revolution was fought
        B. that Marion tricked British troops
        C. that Marion was captured
        D. how many British camps Marion's men raided

_____ **2.** The story suggests that
        A. nylon bristles were first used around A.D. 1500
        B. hog bristles are mostly used now
        C. most people never use toothbrushes
        D. the chew stick did not have bristles

_____ **3.** You cannot tell from the story
        A. how many times Roosevelt was elected
        B. what disease Roosevelt had
        C. where Roosevelt was born
        D. what national office Roosevelt held

_____ **4.** You can conclude that Cora and Floyd
        A. used to live in the country
        B. live in New York City
        C. have many friends
        D. like movies more than museums

_____ **5.** This story suggests that S.E. Hinton
        A. is a teenager
        B. would like to act in movies
        C. no longer writes books
        D. has written more than one book

1. There was war in the Middle East. The country of Israel had just been formed. Its Arab neighbors were upset. Ralph Bunche worked in the State Department of the United States. He was sent to help end the war. Bunche knew the war would not be easy to stop. But at last he gained a peace between the two sides. In 1950 he became the first African American to win the Nobel Peace Prize.

2. The smallest flower on earth is on the duckweed plant. Its blossom can barely be seen with the naked eye. The small duckweed plants float free on still water. These plants are a popular food for ducks.

3. In Aztec legends the new world needed light and warmth. Two sons of the Aztec god wanted to jump into the fire. They wanted to become the sun. The first brother jumped into the fire. He became the sun. But the other brother was afraid. When he jumped into the fire, he became only the moon.

4. Leonardo da Vinci was a great artist. He lived about five hundred years ago. His most famous work is the painting *Mona Lisa*. He also liked to learn about all sorts of things. He knew much about the human body. He loved to invent things, too. He even drew plans for a flying machine.

5. The Iditarod is a sled-dog race across Alaska. Each team has one person to drive the sled and a group of about 12 dogs to pull it. The person, called a musher, rides on the sled with the food and supplies. The team must cross more than one thousand miles in cold and often snowy weather. It takes about two weeks. The musher puts special socks on each dog's paws. The musher also feeds and cares for the dogs on the long ride. The dogs run fast and pull the musher all the way to the finish line.

_____ **1.** You can tell from the story that Bunche
   A. worked for the Israeli government
   B. was honored for his hard work
   C. solved the Middle East conflict easily
   D. did not go to the Middle East

_____ **2.** From the story you <u>cannot</u> tell
   A. on what plant the smallest flower grows
   B. what animal likes to eat the duckweed plant
   C. how small these flowers are
   D. what color the smallest flowers are

_____ **3.** The story suggests that
   A. fear kept one brother from becoming the sun
   B. the Aztec god had five sons
   C. only one brother jumped into the fire
   D. the first brother never jumped into the fire

_____ **4.** You <u>cannot</u> tell from the story
   A. when Leonardo lived
   B. the name of Leonardo's most famous painting
   C. if Leonardo's flying machine could fly
   D. that Leonardo was a famous painter

_____ **5.** The story tells that
   A. mushers and their dogs work together to finish
      the race
   B. sled dogs take care of themselves during the race
   C. mushers don't worry about the sled dogs
   D. mushers and dogs ride on the sled together

1. Cochise was a great chief of the Apache tribe. His people often had trouble with settlers in the Southwest. Cochise was captured by soldiers under a flag of truce. He was charged with a crime he did not commit. But Cochise escaped. For ten years he led attacks on soldiers and settlers. But Cochise was captured once more. He was then forced to live on a reservation.

2. The smallest bird on earth is the bee hummingbird. When it is fully grown, it weighs only one tenth of an ounce. It is only about two inches long. Its nest is the size of a walnut shell.

3. The average life span of an American is now 76 years. Most other creatures do not live as long. Dogs and cats live about 13 years. A horse can live up to 30 years. A robin has a life span of about 12 years. A goldfish can live more than 20 years. A box turtle has the longest life span. It can live more than 100 years.

4. Did you know that your body shrinks as the day goes by? When you wake up, you are your tallest. Your body is relaxed. Your muscles are stretched, and your joints are limber. As the day passes, your muscles tighten. Gravity pulls down on your body, too. Your body may be an inch shorter by the end of the day.

5. Florence Nightingale was born into a rich family. She could have lived an easy life. But she wanted a life of service. She began working as a nurse. Soon she was an expert on hospitals. At the time they were dirty and badly managed. She worked hard for hospital reforms. Then she worked as a nurse during the Crimean War. She worked long hours to help wounded soldiers. Her efforts earned her a special name. She became known as the Lady of the Lamp.

_____ **1.** You <u>cannot</u> tell from the story
    A. how many times Cochise was captured
    B. what tribe Cochise belonged to
    C. how long Cochise led attacks on soldiers
    D. where Cochise's reservation was located

_____ **2.** You can tell that the bee hummingbird
    A. is very big
    B. has a very small nest
    C. weighs very much
    D. cannot fly

_____ **3.** From this story you can tell that
    A. a box turtle lives longer than an American
    B. a horse lives longer than an American
    C. a goldfish lives longer than a box turtle
    D. an American lives longer than a box turtle

_____ **4.** The story does <u>not</u> tell
    A. why your body shrinks during the day
    B. how much your weight changes as you sleep
    C. the time during the day when you are tallest
    D. how much your body can shrink during the day

_____ **5.** From this story you can tell
    A. when the Crimean War took place
    B. that Nightingale knew little about hospitals
    C. how Nightingale got her nickname
    D. that Nightingale was always poor

1. It is almost spring. Latwanda is not looking forward to the change of season. That is because some flowering plants make her sick. In the spring the air is full of pollens. When Latwanda starts sneezing, her friends know that spring is here.

2. Tina called her friend Eva in Maryland. Eva sounded very sleepy when she said hello. The two girls talked for ten minutes. Then Eva said she had to go. "School starts early, you know," she said. "I need my sleep." It was then that Tina knew what she had done. She forgot that Maryland's time zone was not the same as California's.

3. There are more than six billion people on Earth. But scientists think there are four billion insects in each square mile of land. That means there are more than 150 million insects for each person. But very few insects harm people.

4. Stars do not last forever. After billions of years, they just burn out. Some stars suddenly brighten before they dim. These stars are called novas. *Nova* means "new" in Latin. The novas seem to be new stars. The last great nova was in 1054. It could be seen even in the daytime. It outshone everything in the sky except the sun and moon.

5. Mary Bethune had a dream. She wanted to start a school for African American children. She had a teaching degree. But she had no building. And she had no money. Still Mary had hope. She received donations. At last her school opened in 1904. Through her hard work, the school was a big success. It became known as Bethune-Cookman College. The school, located in Florida, is still open.

1. This story suggests that
   A. Latwanda catches colds from her friends
   B. pollens make Latwanda sneeze
   C. dust mites make Latwanda sneeze
   D. medicine helps Latwanda get well

2. You can conclude from the story that
   A. Eva did not enjoy talking to Tina
   B. Tina did not enjoy talking to Eva
   C. Tina and Eva talk often on the phone
   D. Eva was asleep when Tina called

3. This story does not tell
   A. how many people are on Earth
   B. how many insects are in each square mile
   C. which insects are most dangerous to people
   D. how many more insects there are than people

4. You can tell from the story that
   A. novas are not seen very often
   B. great novas happen all the time
   C. all stars become novas
   D. the nova of 1054 was not very bright

5. The story does not tell
   A. what Mary Bethune's dream was
   B. when Mary Bethune's school opened
   C. where Mary Bethune's school was located
   D. who gave Mary Bethune donations

1. Several large earthquakes have happened in the United States. They have caused much damage. The strongest earthquake in the United States happened in Missouri. It took place in 1811. The center of the earthquake was near a town called New Madrid. Since few people lived near this town, nobody was killed. But the earthquake was quite strong. It changed the course of the Mississippi River.

2. The game of lacrosse was first played by the Iroquois. It was a very rough game. Up to 1,000 men took part. There were 500 on each side. Now it is played with only 10 players on each side.

3. There was a big race to reach the North Pole. Several teams of explorers wanted to get there first. One team was led by Robert Peary. On his team was an African American named Matthew Henson. Henson drove the lead dog sled. His sled moved out ahead of the others. Across the frozen land he raced. On a cold morning in 1909, Henson stood at the top of the world. He became the first man to reach the North Pole.

4. The largest flower on Earth can be found in Indonesia. It is called the giant rafflesia. This flower can grow up to three feet wide. It can weigh up to 15 pounds. But the flower is not very pretty. It has scales instead of petals. And it gives off a bad smell.

5. The Grand Canyon is found in Arizona. It is a gorge about one mile deep. The gorge is over two hundred miles long. Its width varies from 4 to 18 miles. The Colorado River runs through it. The canyon has been forming for millions of years. Much of the canyon was formed by erosion.

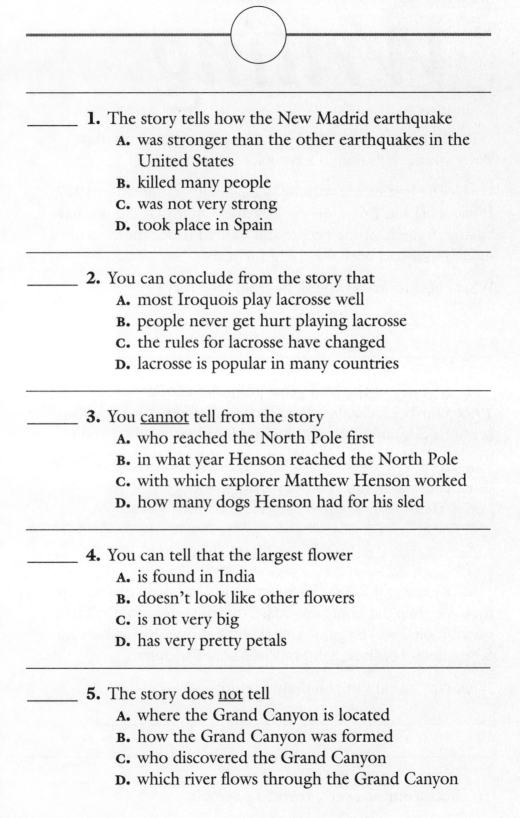

_____ **1.** The story tells how the New Madrid earthquake
  A. was stronger than the other earthquakes in the United States
  B. killed many people
  C. was not very strong
  D. took place in Spain

_____ **2.** You can conclude from the story that
  A. most Iroquois play lacrosse well
  B. people never get hurt playing lacrosse
  C. the rules for lacrosse have changed
  D. lacrosse is popular in many countries

_____ **3.** You <u>cannot</u> tell from the story
  A. who reached the North Pole first
  B. in what year Henson reached the North Pole
  C. with which explorer Matthew Henson worked
  D. how many dogs Henson had for his sled

_____ **4.** You can tell that the largest flower
  A. is found in India
  B. doesn't look like other flowers
  C. is not very big
  D. has very pretty petals

_____ **5.** The story does <u>not</u> tell
  A. where the Grand Canyon is located
  B. how the Grand Canyon was formed
  C. who discovered the Grand Canyon
  D. which river flows through the Grand Canyon

Writing

Read each story. Think about a conclusion you can draw. Write your conclusion in a complete sentence.

1. The first movie with people talking was shown in 1927. It was a big hit. But some movies made after that did not have talking in them. Some people still wanted to see the kind of movies they had been watching for years.

What conclusion can you draw from this story?

_____

_____

2. A family in England got a goldfish in 1956. It lived until 1999. One book claims it lived longer than any other goldfish kept in a fish tank. But who knows? Some people may want to keep the age of their goldfish a secret.

What conclusion can you draw from this story?

_____

_____

3. By the year 2000, 34 Super Bowls had been played. This football game draws big crowds. But many more football fans watch it on TV. The game that had the most TV watchers was Super Bowl 16. In it, San Francisco beat Cincinnati.

What conclusion can you draw from this story?

_____

_____

To check your answers, turn to page 60.

Read the story below. What conclusions can you draw? Use the clues in the story to answer the questions in complete sentences.

Raul is from Cuba. He came to America with his mom. At first they lived in Florida. Raul liked Florida, so he did not want to move. But his mom found out she had an uncle in New Jersey. He helped her find a good job. So Raul and his mom moved in with Raul's grand-uncle. Raul went to high school. There he got a surprise. Many of the students were Cuban Americans. They spoke Spanish and English. Raul decided he was going to like New Jersey.

1. Was Raul born in America? How do you know?

_____

_____

2. When Raul lived in Cuba, did he meet his grand-uncle? How do you know?

_____

_____

3. Do Raul and his mom live alone? How do you know?

_____

_____

4. Does Raul want to move back to Florida? How do you know?

_____

_____

To check your answers, turn to page 60.

Check Yourself

Using What You Know, Page 3
1. a zebra **2.** an elephant **3.** a giraffe **4.** a dolphin

Practice Drawing Conclusions, Page 4
2. C

To check your answers to pages 6–29, see page 61.

Writing, Page 30
Possible answers include:

1. No women voted for Rankin.

2. At first there was only one kind of softball game.

3. Mr. Jones is the bus driver.

Writing, Page 31
Possible answers include:

1. Laree was visiting her grandmother. She got off the plane.

2. She is a student. She is planning to call her school friends.

3. The Tytanic is a water ride. Laree thinks she might get soaked.

4. Laree's friends don't live near her grandmother. They live at least four hours away.

To check your answers to pages 32–57, see page 62.

Writing, Page 58
Possible answers include:

1. Movies didn't always have talking.

2. The English family's goldfish was at least 43 years old.

3. Most people who see the Super Bowl watch it on TV.

Writing, Page 59
Possible answers include:

1. Raul was not born in America. He came to America from Cuba.

2. Raul did not meet his grand-uncle in Cuba. He found out about his grand-uncle after he moved to Florida.

3. Raul and his mom don't live alone. They live with Raul's grand-uncle.

4. Raul probably doesn't want to move back to Florida. He thinks he will like New Jersey.

Steck-Vaughn • Comprehension Skills Series

Check Yourself

Unit 1 pp. 6–7	Unit 2 pp. 8–9	Unit 3 pp. 10–11	Unit 4 pp. 12–13	Unit 5 pp. 14–15	Unit 6 pp. 16–17	Unit 7 pp. 18–19	Unit 8 pp. 20–21	Unit 9 pp. 22–23	Unit 10 pp. 24–25	Unit 11 pp. 26–27	Unit 12 pp. 28–29
1. C	1. B	1. B	1. B	1. C	1. A	1. C	1. A	1. B	1. A	1. C	1. C
2. B	2. C	2. A	2. C	2. A	2. A	2. B	2. A	2. B	2. B	2. B	2. D
3. C	3. A	3. C	3. B	3. C	3. A	3. A	3. C	3. B	3. C	3. C	3. A
4. C	4. C	4. A	4. D	4. B	4. B	4. B	4. C	4. C	4. A	4. A	4. B
5. D	5. C	5. B	5. B	5. A	5. C	5. D	5. C	5. A	5. B	5. C	5. D

Unit 13 pp. 32–33	Unit 14 pp. 34–35	Unit 15 pp. 36–37	Unit 16 pp. 38–39	Unit 17 pp. 40–41	Unit 18 pp. 42–43	Unit 19 pp. 44–45	Unit 20 pp. 46–47	Unit 21 pp. 48–49	Unit 22 pp. 50–51	Unit 23 pp. 52–53	Unit 24 pp. 54–55	Unit 25 pp. 56–57
1. C	1. C	1. A	1. A	1. D	1. C	1. A	1. B	1. B	1. B	1. D	1. B	1. A
2. A	2. D	2. C	2. D	2. C	2. B	2. B	2. D	2. D	2. D	2. B	2. D	2. C
3. B	3. C	3. D	3. C	3. A	3. D	3. D	3. A	3. C	3. A	3. A	3. C	3. D
4. D	4. A	4. D	4. B	4. B	4. C	4. C	4. B	4. A	4. C	4. B	4. A	4. B
5. C	5. B	5. D	5. D	5. C	5. A	5. D	5. C	5. D	5. A	5. C	5. D	5. C